Original title:
Fables of the Fern Forest

Copyright © 2025 Creative Arts Management OÜ
All rights reserved.

Author: Fiona Harrington
ISBN HARDBACK: 978-1-80567-445-0
ISBN PAPERBACK: 978-1-80567-744-4

## The Enchanted Thicket

In a thicket where giggles bloom,
A squirrel dances, shaking his broom.
The rabbits chuckle, wearing hats,
As each one sneezes, the others go splat!

A raccoon juggles acorns with flair,
While a sleepy snail clings to a chair.
The wise old owl hoots a loud cheer,
'Join in the fun, my friends, have no fear!'

## **Nightfall in the Leafy Realm**

As night falls, the shadows play tricks,
A hedgehog's giggle, a slippery fix.
Fireflies twinkle, lighting up smiles,
While frogs croak tunes from cool, mossy aisles.

The moon peeks through leaves, shining bright,
As raccoons start a conga delight.
They dance in circles, all wild and free,
While crickets join in with their symphony!

## Songs of the Sunlit Clearing

In a clearing where sunbeams fling,
Birds gossip 'bout a new peacock king.
The butterflies flutter, in colors so bold,
While hiccuping bees share tales that they've told.

A friendly deer tries to sing with the crowd,
But her voice quivers, she's not feeling proud.
All of them chuckle, and soon join the tune,
As laughter rises, like flowers in June.

## The Wisdom of the Old Oak

An ancient oak, with wrinkles galore,
Hears the squirrels plotting mischief galore.
'Steal the farmer's carrots!' they hatch a fine plot,
But the oak just chuckles, 'Oh, what a lot!

A fox wanders by with a grin on his snout,
'Listen closely, my friends, here's what's it's about:
Gloating leads to slipping, and slipping leads to falls,
So stick to your squabbles, ignore the tall walls!'

## In the Heart of the Hidden Hollow

In a glen where the squirrels play,
A chatty frog lost his way.
He hopped up high, then fell down low,
Said, "I wish I could just grow!"

The raccoons laughed, they found it grand,
As the frog flopped like he was banned.
They built a tower of acorn stacks,
But the frog got stuck, and that was that!

A wise old owl gave a grin,
"To leap above, you must begin!"
With one big bounce, he hit a branch,
And all the critters joined to dance.

Now they gather when dusk falls,
Frog tells tales of his brave calls.
In the hollow, laughter reigns,
As stories dance through leafy lanes.

## Rooted in Forgotten Whispers

In a patch where wild onions grow,
Lived a raccoon who loved to show.
When eating snacks, he'd wear a cape,
Declared, "I'm a knight who'll change my shape!"

The trees would chuckle, the vines would sway,
As he spun around, hip-hip-hooray!
His bag of tricks was quite a sight,
Filled with goodies that shone so bright.

One day a fox, sleek and sly,
Challenged the knight, aiming to try.
With cunning moves and a bit of flair,
The knight danced circles in midair!

After a tumble, they both fell down,
Laughter echoed all around town.
In forgotten whispers, joy arose,
From raccoon knights in comic prose.

## Breath of the Breezy Boughs

In the high branches, a squirrel took flight,
Chasing his acorns, he danced with delight.
A twist and a turn, oh! What a grand show,
But he slipped on a leaf and fell with a 'whoa!'

The old owl just chuckled, with wisdom to spare,
'Life's like a nut; sometimes it's rare.'
The breeze blew a tune, all the trees swayed low,
And laughed at the antics of the sprightly show.

## Tales Told by Timeworn Trunks

Beneath a great trunk, a beetle did boast,
'I'm the fastest around!' he claimed with a toast.
But a sloth heard the chatter, with a grin he declared,
'Dear friend, I'll beat you—if I just got prepared!'

The chorus of laughter rose high from the glade,
As the beetle zipped off, the sloth just delayed.
'Maybe next time,' the bugs chimed in cheer,
'You'll learn slow and steady wins most of the year!'

## The Moonlit Market of Creatures

Under the moonlight, critters set up stalls,
With glowing green apples and sparkling pink balls.
The raccoon was bartering, 'Come take a look!'
Where to find that shiny new fishy cookbook?

A hedgehog sold snacks made from berries and thyme,
While the tortoise played music, keeping perfect time.
Each creature joined in, sharing laughter and cheer,
In the market of friends, there's nothing to fear!

## The Roots That Hold Secrets

Down by the roots, the whispers were loud,
A gossiping fungus spoke to the crowd.
'Did you hear about Fern? She wore a new hat!
Said it was woven by that old chatty cat!'

The roots held their secrets, twisted and tangled,
While mushrooms all giggled, their laughter wrangled.
For in this snug forest, with all its sweet quirks,
Even the silence is full of fun works.

## Echoes where Elders Stand

Beneath the moss, the old trees grin,
They hide the secrets of where we've been.
Squirrels gossip in the soft, cool shade,
Telling tales of mischief, unafraid.

A frog in a suit, so dapper and bright,
Claims he's the king of the forest delight.
With a twirl and a hop, he bursts into song,
Others join in, it won't be long!

## Constellations Among the Canopy

Fireflies dance like stars in the night,
Illuminating fables with their twinkling light.
A hedgehog debates with a wise old owl,
Their laughter echoes through the woods, with a growl.

The raccoons are pirates, with a treasure so bold,
Finding shiny trinkets, they never grow old.
Each night's an adventure, with humor galore,
In the canopy's arms, who could ask for more?

## **Leafy Legends of Lost Time**

Acorns wear crowns in a gathering waltz,
While mushrooms play poker, amidst giggles and halts.
A squirrel shares tales of a thief in the mist,
Who nabbed all the nuts—oh, can you resist?

And then there's the rabbit, a legend, a hoot,
Whose dance is so clumsy, he falls on his boot.
With every misstep, the laughter compiles,
In this leafy realm, joy is always in styles.

## The Spiral Path of Forgotten Dreams


A snail dreams slowly of races to win,
While chipmunks all cheer for their friend with a grin.
They gather round stories of journeys so grand,
And laugh 'til they ache, in this mystical land.

A wise old tortoise, who knows every trick,
Teaches life lessons in a manner quite slick.
With giggles and grins, they traverse the terrain,
Finding joy in the paths where dreams never wane.

## The Threads that Bind Us

In the forest where giggles roam,
A squirrel spun tales of a gnome.
With threads of mischief, they did weave,
A cloak of laughter, hard to believe.

A rabbit hopped in, his ears so tall,
He tripped on a root and began to sprawl.
The gnome just chuckled, a warm delight,
They stitched a friendship by whim's light.

## **Moonlit Rhapsody in the Hollow**


Beneath the moon's cheeky, glowing grin,
A raccoon danced, shedding his skin.
With shadows prancing, a merry sight,
He serenaded the owls with delight.

A badger joined in with a tap and a spin,
Creating a night where giggles begin.
In a hollow of whispers, they jived so free,
The forest echoed with their jubilee.

## The Tapestry of Time in the Wild

In a glade where the ticks of time play tricks,
A turtle claimed he could do quick flicks.
He spun in circles, quite out of pace,
While the fox laughed, rolling on his face.

Then came a breeze, with a snort and a puff,
It tangled their tails, saying, 'That's enough!'
With threads of laughter, they wove the night,
A tapestry bright with their silly plight.

## A Chance Encounter in the Glade


By accident, a hedgehog met a hare,
They both jumped back, startled in the air.
'You thought I was a shrub!' the hare did tease,
'Well, you're prickly!' said hedgehog, 'Do be at ease!'

In laughter they fell, rolling on the floor,
Making friends in a way they hadn't planned before.
In the glade where stories and chuckles combine,
They found camaraderie, oh how divine!

## The Forest Floor's Storyteller

In shadows deep where whispers play,
A toad sings tales at the end of day.
Beneath the blooms, he cracks a joke,
While beetles laugh till they choke.

A squirrel nods with a wiggly tail,
As raccoons join with a raucous wail.
The owls look down from their lofty posts,
Chuckling softly at the lively hosts.

Mice scurry round, a comedic crew,
Planned their dance with a pie on cue.
They stumble and tumble with rhythmic grace,
What a sight, in this merry place!

So gather 'round for a forest show,
Where every bark and chirp steals the show.
With giggles and chuckles, hearts bloom bright,
In the laughter of dusk, all feels just right.

## Twilight Beneath the Canopy

As twilight falls and shadows dance,
A chipmunk dons a top hat by chance.
He bows with flair, as fireflies cheer,
While crickets debate if they should draw near.

A frog hops in with a twirly smile,
Claiming he'll sing in the grandest style.
But notes go wibbly, then crash like a tune,
The forest erupts; it's a glorious boon!

An owl who hoots like a croaky song,
Wants to join in, though he's quite wrong.
With every verse, the chaos grows,
And laughter's the nectar that each creature knows.

So gather here in the twilight's embrace,
As stories unfold in this humorous space.
Where lighthearted spirits frolic and sing,
In the canopy's glow, happiness takes wing.

## Serpent's Slumber Amongst the Ferns

A snake coils tight, dreaming flat,
Of grand adventures wearing a hat.
He twirls and sways in his verdant nest,
While snoring softly, he thinks he's the best.

His ferns giggle as they sway along,
Joining a chorus, they hum a tune strong.
"Oh what a dancer!" they whisper with glee,
Unaware he's just dreaming beneath the old tree.

A lizard creeps up with a sly little grin,
To join in the fun, though he's wearing thin.
With a wobbly leap, he trips on a leaf,
Causing a ruckus, oh what a relief!

So while the serpent snoozes away,
The forest awakens to frolic and play.
In laughter and smiles, their joy takes flight,
Creating a world where dreams feel just right.

## Echoing Legends of the Lost

In the heart of the woods where legends talk,
A funky raccoon takes his nightly walk.
With a hat so tall and shoes too bright,
He claims to see fairies take flight.

But each tale grows bigger with every tell,
From owls who gossip about a wishing well.
A hedgehog rolls by, snagging the scene,
Saying, "I'm the sprightliest you've ever seen!"

Once a squirrel skated on leaves with flair,
To impress the forest, but fell in despair.
Now he juggles acorns, his new-found art,
While onlookers giggle; they love every part.

So gather and hear as the stories unfold,
Of creatures, mishaps, and legends bold.
In laughter and joy, the forest's array,
In echoes of fun, we all find our way.

## Tales Woven in Green

In a grove where the crickets play,
A squirrel stole the pie today.
With a wink and a swish, he took a dash,
Leaving behind a trail of trash!

The owls grinned, giving him a shout,
'You can't eat that, you silly lout!'
But the squirrel just laughed, quick as a fox,
While the pie sat grumpy, in a box.

The mushrooms giggled, colors so bright,
As he danced away into the night.
Nature chuckled with all its might,
Watching the thief scamper with delight.

So if you're in the woods, take a glance,
You might see him trying to prance.
But remember the wise won't get too near,
To a pie-loving squirrel who's full of cheer!

## The Dance of the Wildflowers

Beneath the sun, the petals twirled,
A funny sight in the green world.
Daisies whispered, 'Let's spin around!'
While the roses just rolled on the ground.

The bees buzzed in, with a jittery beat,
As the wildflowers picked up their feet.
They swayed and dipped, in a playful spree,
While butterflies joined, with glee and tea!

The tulips tried to lead the show,
But fell over, racing too slow.
Laughter erupted from every leaf,
As nature giggled in disbelief.

So if you stroll through fields so nice,
Don't miss the flowers in their dance twice.
For they hold secrets in every bloom,
And laughter echoes in nature's room!

## Echoes of the Burbling Brook

A brook bubbled softly, tales to share,
It chortled and chuckled, without a care.
With frogs on rocks, it told of the past,
While fish in the water swam by so fast.

The pebbles listened, wide-eyed and round,
Murmurs and giggles filled the ground.
'That snail thinks he's speedy, just look at him!'
They all burst out laughing; it was a whim!

The brook splashed joyfully, water in tow,
Tickling the roots, where daisies grow.
Each ripple a giggle, each wave a smile,
Telling funny tales all the while.

So if you wander, listen real close,
To the brook's little tales, they matter the most.
In its happy burble, find a laugh,
For nature spins jokes, that's the craft!

## Guardians of the Mossy Path

On the mossy path where the whispers dwell,
Tiny creatures plot a funny spell.
A hedgehog wearing a hat, quite dapper,
Stumbled on mushrooms, oh what a clapper!

The rabbits giggled as he took a spin,
Falling down softly, with a goofy grin.
'This is the most stylish I've ever looked!'
They winked at each other, laughter cooked!

A wise old tortoise chuckled nearby,
'You've got style, but my, oh my!'
He watched the fun unfold with glee,
As critters enjoyed their silly spree.

So if you tread where the moss is thick,
Be careful, or you'll trip, and that'll be slick!
Laughter echoes through branches high,
Guardians in green, under the sky!

## Sandals of the Silent Sprig

In a glade where shadows creep,
The silent sprig danced in sleep.
With sandals bright, it twirled and spun,
Chasing the laughter just for fun.

A squirrel watched with a bead of sweat,
Daring to bet on a friendly duet.
But as the sprig leapt high in glee,
It tripped on moss and fell like a tree!

## In the Embrace of Elderberries

Beneath the bush, berries did sway,
A plump little fox was on display.
'Elderberry pie!' he thought with flair,
While sneaky squirrels stole his share.

The fox cried out, 'Oh my dear friends,
Don't gobble my treats; this fun never ends!'
But rodents just winked and grinned with delight,
For sharing is caring in their berry fight!

## The Song of the Swaying Ferns

In the glen where whispers loom,
The ferns sang softly, dispelling gloom.
They swayed so low with quirky grace,
While frogs joined in with a funny bass.

With tunes that hopped and echoes bright,
The fireflies twinkled in pure delight.
But a twig snapped loud; silence fell fast,
As all held breath for the bashful blast!

## Blossoms on the Breeze's Breath

The flowers giggled in the breeze,
Tickled by whispers of buzzing bees.
They danced with petals that shimmered wide,
And jostled for space, side by side.

A blossom bloomed with a jolly thrum,
It shouted, 'Hey, let's invite some fun!'
But with one big shake, the dance took flight,
And petals were scattered all through the night!

## Whispers Beneath the Canopy

Squirrels plot with acorn hats,
A council held on ten-foot mats.
They laugh and tease the passing deer,
As breezes blow and critters jeer.

Frogs play cards on lily pads,
While turtles avoid the gabbing lads.
Chirping crickets sing the tune,
Of antics held beneath the moon.

## The Sage of the Ancient Trees

A wise old oak once shared a joke,
That left all creatures quite bespoke.
"It's hard to leaf when roots are deep,
So take a break and don't lose sleep!"

The chipmunks giggled, lost their nut,
Too busy rolling in the rut.
The sage just chuckled, rolled his eyes,
While humming tunes that mock the skies.

## Shadows of the Woodland Spirits

Elusive sprites wear leaves for hats,
They dance with joy while dodging bats.
Their giggles echo through the night,
In shadows churned by fading light.

They sprinkle mischief on the ground,
And chase the lost, who whirl around.
With tiny feet and silly grins,
They paint the world with playful sins.

## Secrets in the Underbrush

Beneath the thorns, the gossip flies,
Of tiny mice and startled cries.
A hedgehog winks, a rabbit sighs,
To share the tales of sweet surprise.

The beetles march in straight-lined rows,
They argue much, as everyone knows.
In hidden nooks, the secrets bloom,
Of laughter lurking in the gloom.

## The Fern's Forgotten Friends

In shadows where the ferns do sway,
A turtle danced to start the play.
The rabbit jumped, then took a fall,
While squirrels laughed, they'd seen it all.

A snail then joined with pace so slow,
Declaring that he'd steal the show.
He slipped and slid right past the tree,
The ferns all giggled, oh so free!

A gathering of oddball friends,
From morning light till evening bends.
They shared their tales of clumsy flair,
And promised more laughs, if you dare!

So when you wander through the glade,
And hear the sounds of pranks well laid,
Remember those who frolic near,
The fern friends, giggling, full of cheer.

## The Blossom's Silent Song

In a garden where the blossoms bloom,
A flower sang without a tune.
Its petals swayed, a silent jest,
As lazy bees took time to rest.

A dandelion puffed out proud,
While tulips whispered 'what a crowd!'
The rose rolled eyes at such a sight,
"Can flowers have fun? Oh, what a night!"

The petals chuckled, soft and sweet,
As ants marched by on tiny feet.
In daytime's glow, they'd laugh and tease,
These blossoms swayed in gentle breeze.

And when the moonlight cast its glow,
The garden twinkled, all aglow.
They shared their stories, one by one,
In dreams of laughter, never done.

## Hidden Hues of the Haunting Hollow

In a hollow where the shadows creep,
Lived colors vibrant, never asleep.
A polka-dot frog in purple shoes,
Sang silly songs with a lopsided croon.

A chameleon teamed up with a crow,
Changing hues with each new show.
"Your jokes are shady," the rabbit cried,
As the hollow chuckled, wide-eyed.

A duo of owls made silly faces,
In the twilight, they found their places.
The trees swayed gently to their tune,
As fireflies danced beneath the moon.

And hidden in laughter, bright, and bold,
This hollow's secrets, forever told.
Where colors clash and humor thrives,
In a realm where funny never dies.

## Leaves that Laughed and Wept

Once there were leaves, with laughter's grace,
Who flitted about a merry chase.
They giggled with every gust of air,
And danced in circles without a care.

But one fell down, with a woeful sigh,
"I wish I could soar and touch the sky!"
The others laughed and spun around,
Saying, "Join the fun on the ground!"

An acorn chuckled, "Come take a chance!
We'll show you how to spin and prance!"
So they twirled and whirled, in joyful heaps,
While one leaf wept, but laughter keeps.

In the end, they found a way,
To mix their joys with tears of play.
For in this world of highs and lows,
Leaves laugh and weep, as friendship grows.

## The Hidden Den of the Forest Folk

In a nook where secrets dwell,
The creatures dance, ring a bell.
Squirrels wear tiny top hats,
Bartering nuts with chattering rats.

They giggle and they plot each day,
While the owls have things to say.
A game of hide-and-seek ensues,
As rabbits wear silly shoes.

The fox brings snacks, all wrapped with care,
While hedgehogs spin tales, full of flair.
With acorns roasted over a fire,
Their laughter lifts the spirits higher.

When moonlight drapes the frisky night,
They toast to friendship, oh what a sight.
In the hidden den, wild and free,
These forest folk share glee endlessly.

## Lament of the Fallen Sapling

A young green sprout, oh what a plight,
With dreams of growing tall and bright.
   But a raccoon stepped on its head,
   Now it sings songs of woe instead.

The wind whispers, "Don't be sad,
You'll still be fine, just a tad mad!"
A nearby oak chuckles with pride,
While the sapling just wants to hide.

Yet bees buzz by with tales of blooms,
And ants march on, sweeping up rooms.
The fallen sapling shakes with mirth,
   Finding joy in this silly earth.

When the rain patters, it sways along,
   Singing a sweet, nutty song.
For in this tale of ups and downs,
Even fallen friends wear crowns.

## Journey through the Twilit Grove

As twilight falls, the fireflies glow,
A raccoon leads, saying, "Follow me, go!"
With twinkling eyes, the path is bright,
Crisp leaves rustle, what a delight!

A hedgehog carries a map, quite bleak,
It shows where to find the best treats to seek.
Through chirps of frogs and hoots of owls,
They wander, sharing giggles and howls.

The mushrooms dance, a merry crew,
Dressed in spots of every hue.
They beckon friends to join the cheer,
In the grove, there's naught to fear.

And when the stars begin to twink,
They gather round for a toast to drink.
Here in the grove, with laughter and fun,
The journey never ends, just begun!

## Curiosities of the Canopied World

Up in the trees, where secrets spin,
The parrots gossip, where to begin?
A toucan with a beak so wide,
Shows off the treasures he can hide.

With lizards strutting under bright leaves,
And all the gossip that the chatter weaves.
The monkeys juggle with joy and flair,
While squirrel acrobats perform in the air.

A feathered hat could go for a date,
But who will win the great match of fate?
The owls ponder with a wise old grin,
"Here in the canopy, where to begin?"

With playful tricks and witty debates,
The forest life celebrates its mates.
In this curious, canopied space,
Every turn brings a new, funny face.

## **Lore of the Twilight Glow**

In a forest where shadows play,
The critters dance at end of day.
A squirrel juggles acorns with flair,
While owls hoot jokes, light as air.

The raccoons plot with clever grins,
Intent on winning, regardless of sins.
A rabbit slips on a banana peel,
And laughter echoes, oh what a deal!

The trees sway to a rhythm so sweet,
As frogs serenade with tap-dancing feet.
A hedgehog twirls, spins round and around,
In the glow of twilight, joy abounds.

With each giggle, the night grows bright,
In the warmth of fun, with pure delight.
The critters know, as the stars will show,
That laughter's the magic in this twilight glow.

## Beneath the Veil of Ferns

Beneath the ferns, a secret play,
Where critters gather when skies turn gray.
A snail tells tales with a dramatic flair,
While a mole pops out to share his hair.

A turtle raced—oh what a sight!
He slipped and slid with all his might.
The ferns gave way to silly schemes,
Invisible paths, like in crazy dreams.

A woodpecker drums to a wacky beat,
While dancing leaves sway with silly feet.
Each creature takes part in this grand parade,
In the laughter of friends, no plans are made.

In the quiet, where mischief grows,
And laughter mingles with evening's prose,
Happiness blooms, like the gleeful ferns,
In the heart of the forest, joy always returns.

## The Flicker of Fireflies

As dusk wraps softly around the trees,
Fireflies flicker, like stars with ease.
A busy ant tries to take flight,
While giggling beetles dance through the night.

A frog croaks jokes that make others snort,
While a hedgehog competes in a silly sport.
With each tiny flash, new laughter ignites,
In the whimsical glow, all worries take flight.

A dragonfly zips by with flair,
Chasing a wink from the cool evening air.
The melodies mesh, as the night unfolds,
Creating memories like tales once told.

Fireflies shine—like an audience bright,
In the comedy show of this joyful night.
With each little blink, they share their delight,
As laughter and glow fill the shadows with light.

## Whimsy in the Whispering Leaves

In the rustling leaves, secrets are spun,
A tiny mouse thinks he's so much fun.
He tells tall tales of great big cheese,
While crickets chirp in the soft evening breeze.

A snake in shades, with a cool swagger,
Slithers past, just a little stagger.
The leaves giggle softly at his grand pose,
As a rabbit in shades strikes a pose with those.

The wise old owl gives a sly grin,
Winking quick, his games begin.
Each leaf joins in the playful tease,
Laughter erupts beneath the trees.

In the night's embrace, playtime begins,
The forest bursts forth with laughter and spins.
In the whimsy of the leaves where fun never leaves,
Joy echoes forever, as everyone believes.

## The Charmed Circle of Creatures

In shadows where the giggles dwell,
Beneath the vibrant green, they tell.
A squirrel danced on tiptoes high,
While frogs croaked tunes that made birds sigh.

The rabbit wore a jaunty hat,
And held a tea party with a rat.
They served up snacks of dandelion,
While bees buzzed sweet, like voices fine.

A turtle flew a paper kite,
That soared and dove, oh what a sight!
With every laugh, the forest spun,
In the charmed circle, all is fun.

So join the frolic, jump and play,
In this enchanted, silly array.
With each new friend, the laughter grows,
In the forest's heart, where joy just flows.

## A Journey through Celestial Canopies

Through leafy paths where giggles soar,
A raccoon dreams by an ancient door.
With starlit tales of flying fish,
And worms who dance near a mushroom dish.

The owls wore glasses, wise and round,
Dictating jokes of the woodland ground.
And squirrels in boots did pirouette,
While falling leaves became a net.

Each branch a stage for curious plays,
Where shadows prance in moonlit rays.
The laughter echoes, a joyful sound,
As critters bounce from tree to ground.

So venture forth, let spirits rise,
In this lush haven beneath the skies.
Twirl with the breeze, lose track of time,
In the celestial laughter, sublime.

## Frosted Fronds and Fables

When frosty ferns wear coats of white,
The cheeky mice plan a snowy night.
They build a castle, a grand delight,
With chewy snacks, it feels just right.

The hedgehog plays the royal guard,
With a toothbrush sword, it's not too hard.
And snowmen come to life with cheer,
Telling tales that all can hear.

A hare in skates takes to the ice,
With spins and tricks, oh so precise.
Each slip and slide brings joyous grins,
In this frosty land, everyone wins.

So gather 'round, let the stories flow,
In frosted fronds where laughter grows.
With each small jest and playful shout,
In winter's charm, there's never doubt.

## Messages Carried by the Wind

The whispers danced on a breezy morn,
As butterflies shared tales of scorn.
A clever crow sent notes with flair,
While chipmunks stopped to laugh and stare.

The wind was bold, it swung around,
Tickling leaves without a sound.
It told of socks that flew from lines,
And gnomes who painted silly signs.

A parrot squawked, "Don't take it slow!"
As windblown waves began to flow.
Through branches swayed with glee, they sang,
With every gust, the laughter sprang.

So lend an ear to what's unsaid,
In messages that the breeze has spread.
From silly tales to secrets shared,
In joyful gusts, our hearts are bared.

## **The Lure of the Lush Labyrinth**

In a maze of green, I lost my way,
The bushes giggled, 'Come here and play!'
A squirrel wore glasses, reading a sign,
The map was upside down, but who cares? I'm fine!

The flowers chattered in colors so bright,
They gossiped and whispered, oh what a sight!
A snail in a shell claimed to be a prince,
Turns out, he just needed a little more rinse.

I danced with a beetle, he taught me a jig,
Then bumped into mushrooms, all laughing big.
The path twisted round like a silly old game,
But in this green maze, nothing's ever the same!

With vines hanging low like a jester's fine gear,
Each corner held laughter, each step I'd cheer.
The lure was the fun in this leafy terrain,
A nature-made stage where joy would reign!

## Murmurs from the Mossy Mound

On a soft, green mound where moss likes to grow,
Whispers floated up, 'Come join the show!'
A worm dressed in silk said, 'I'm quite the star,'
He wiggled and giggled, my, how bizarre!

Tiny ants marched by with a drum and a bass,
They danced to a tune in this fuzzy-lit space.
A frog in a bowtie croaked poetry sweet,
With lines that would make anyone tap their feet.

The brook played the flute, with splashes and swirls,
While beetles formed circles, inviting the girls.
"Come one, come all!" the mossy mound cried,
In this merry land, with friends by my side.

Laughter and music filled the warm air,
In this mossy retreat, naught a worry or care.
The murmurs of joy nestled deep in the ground,
In nature's green haven, happiness found!

## Spirits of the Sun-Dappled Glade

In a glade where the sun shines, spirits all roam,
Fairies in tutus decided to foam!
With bubbles and giggles, they floated around,
A dance-party here, oh what glee did abound!

A raccoon in shades strutted with flair,
Claiming he's famous, the star of the air.
He slid down a log, did flips—oh so slick,
With laughter that echoed, he felt like the trick!

The flowers all swayed like they knew the beat,
While birds chirped in chorus, tap-dancing their feet.
A hedgehog in boots shared tales from the skies,
Of adventures he had with his bushy-tailed spies.

In this sunny glade, joy is always at play,
With spirits so merry, they brighten the day.
The glimmers of laughter dance under the trees,
In this magical spot, you will feel such a breeze!

## The Weaving of Wisps

In the nighttime woods where the shadows prance,
Wisps spun their tales, taking you to dance.
With twinkling eyes, they laughed, oh so spry,
A riot of tales as they floated on by.

They whispered of gnomes who played tricks on the trees,
And fairies who snickered as they danced in the breeze.
An owl joined the party, so wise and so old,
Telling secrets of dreams and their many-fold gold.

A bobcat in pajamas rolled in with a grin,
Saying, "Take a seat, let the fun now begin!"
With tails that were woven like threads in the night,
They spun webs of laughter, oh what a delight!

So join in the magic, let worries all drift,
In the weaving of wisps, together we lift.
With laughter as bright as the moon up above,
This wild, silly world fills our hearts full of love!

## Scrolls Beneath the Forest Floor

In the damp earth secrets lay,
Excited bugs dance and sway.
A squirrel drops his acorn stash,
While hedgehogs giggle, making a splash.

The mushrooms hum a silly tune,
As crickets play on afternoon.
The wise old toad rolls on a log,
Chasing shadows, what a gag!

A fox in spectacles reads aloud,
Tales of mischief, oh so proud!
And if you peek beneath the leaves,
You'll spot a rabbit who just deceives.

So tread with joy, and don't be shy,
In laughter's arms, let your worries fly.
For beneath the forest, what a show,
Where giggles bloom and friendships grow.

## The Oracle of Old Oaks

Beneath the branches, wise and grand,
The Oracle gives advice unplanned.
With acorns tossed like crystal balls,
He offers wisdom, makes us all fall.

A peacock struts with feathers bright,
Claiming he sees both day and night.
The squirrels chuckle, their tails a-fluff,
"Old Oak, your wisdom's pretty tough!"

The owl hoots out a quirky rhyme,
With words that slip just out of time.
"I predict a snack for you today,
If you are bold and dance away!"

So gather round and lend an ear,
The old tree knows, it's crystal clear.
With roots in humor and leaves in cheer,
His tales will bring you laughter near.

## The Wisdom in the Wildflowers

In a field where daisies twirl and play,
A bustling bee leads the way.
"Why so serious?" he buzzes loud,
"Join the dance, come be proud!"

Tulips gossip and lilies laugh,
Sharing secrets in a flowery craft.
"Did you hear about the clumsy bee?
He tripped on a petal, what a spree!"

The violets crown a bumblebee king,
Crowning him with a daisy ring.
He buzzes proudly, his eyes aglow,
Winging around with a silly show.

As the sun dips low, colors ignite,
Whispers of petals spark pure delight.
In wildflower wisdom, joy is sown,
A tapestry of laughter, brightly grown.

## A Rooted Reverie

In a tangle of roots where the gophers play,
Beneath the earth, they dream away.
With twinkling eyes and floppy ears,
They share their hopes, they share their fears.

A wise old tortoise plods along,
Singing softly a tortoise song.
"Slow and steady wins the race,
But who cares when there's fun to chase?"

The snails gather for a fashion show,
With shells adorned and hearts aglow.
"Who's the fastest?" they tease and poke,
As giggles ripple with every joke.

So let your worries drift away,
Join the critters in their playful fray.
For in the forest, where roots entwine,
Life's a party, sweet and fine.

## Threads of Silence in the thickets

In the thickets where whispers twist,
A squirrel juggles nuts with a flick of his wrist.
They giggle and chatter, the bugs in a line,
As the leaves wave hello, feeling rather divine.

The owl snoozes deep in a leafy cocoon,
Dreaming of romances with the light of the moon.
A rabbit hops past, with pros and with cons,
It's hard to be quiet when you wear such long paws.

The ants form a band, with a twig for a flute,
Singing songs of the berries and their plump, juicy fruit.
With each tiny step, they tap out a beat,
Crickets join in, making the night oh so sweet.

So wander through thickets, where laughter is found,
Amongst all the chatter, let joy be unbound.
For silence may reign, but fun is the thread,
In the winks and the giggles that linger ahead.

## The Chronicles of the Canopied Creatures

High in branches, the critters convene,
With gossip so juicy, it's quite the scene.
A raccoon with tales, he's the life of the show,
With a paw on his chin, he's the star of the flow.

The birds, they bicker about who can fly,
While squirrels debate on the merits of pie.
A snail tells a story of speed and of grace,
While the frogs croak in laughter, keeping up the pace.

Mice form a choir, their voices a buzz,
Singing of mushrooms that grow just because.
While shadows sneak in, like whispers of mist,
The laughter ignites, and no one can resist.

So join the festivities under the sun,
Where creatures are quirky and joy has some fun.
In the canopies' embrace, let your worries unfreeze,
In chronicles woven with giggles and breeze.

## The Unraveled Tale of Twisting Vines

Among twisting vines that bend and weave,
A chameleon grins, oh, can't you believe?
He changes his colors, a painter in flight,
But can't find his socks, oh, what a plight!

The lizards race past, on a slippery course,
Tail-tangling antics become their discourse.
A turtle rolls dice, his luck running thin,
While snickering frogs leap to see who can spin.

The jungle's alive with characters wild,
Each creature a comedian, nature's own child.
With a vine for a swing, they shriek and they dive,
In the game of the forest, oh, isn't it live?

So gather your laughter and dance to the show,
In a world of mischief where giggles just flow.
As tales unravel, let joy intertwine,
In the twists and the turns of the winding vine.

## The Secret Keepers of the Shade

In the cool, dark shade where secrets reside,
A wise old fox watches the world go outside.
He winks at the mice with all their bright tales,
While the frogs and the gnats share scandalous trails.

The raccoons conspire with eyes filled with gleam,
Plotting mischief by the light of a dream.
While butterflies gossip about fashion and flair,
The bees buzz along, with stories to share.

A hidden assembly of creatures unique,
Whispers of wonders and playful mystique.
The shadows may hold tales untold in the air,
But in the laughter and fun, there's joy everywhere.

So pop into shade, where the chuckles connect,
With secret keepers armed with humor perfect.
For laughter is currency in this leafy brigade,
And the joy of the shade is forever displayed.

## Tenders of the Trellis

In a garden so grand, with plants that dance,
Tiny creatures plot their mischief at a glance.
Squirrels in tuxedos, all ready to tease,
Swapping the seeds for some nutty cheese.

The flowers are gossiping, petals a-flutter,
The roses tell tales of a sneaky nut butter.
While bees wear top hats, buzzing with flair,
Spreading sweet rumors through fragrant air.

The vines make a jungle, all tangled and spry,
With sprightly green critters that leap and fly.
They giggle and wiggle, a playful parade,
For laughter is growing, in sunshine and shade.

In this merry haven, so lively and bright,
The garden thrives wild, a joyful sight.
Each tendril and leaf sings a silly refrain,
In the trellis, they'll party, again and again.

## The Shimmering Shade's Secret

Underneath the tall trees, there's a keen whisper,
Of grasshoppers sharing their wild summer jester.
They wear tiny crowns made of shiny dew,
Trading sweet secrets, oh what could they do?

The mushrooms are giggling, all dotted with spots,
While lizards play poker, just using their thoughts.
A rabbit, quite dapper, drags carrots in line,
A banquet of laughter, all yours and all mine.

In the shadows, the critters enjoy their grand feast,
With treats of fine berries, they're joyful, at least.
The moonlight's a spotlight, it dances around,
As laughter and shenanigans leap from the ground.

The secret of giggles in shimmering shade,
Could bring even grumpies some fun and good trade.
So gather the friends, and your joy will be bright,
In the glimmering glade, every heart takes flight.

## Glimpses into the Green Abyss

Peeking through the foliage, what do we see?
A band of mischievous ants having a spree.
In hats made of petals they wiggle with glee,
Turning a simple march into a grand jubilee.

The toads in their jackets, so dapper and spry,
Sing solos of shenanigans under the sky.
While the wise old owl hoots a raucous applause,
For the antics of creatures with no set of laws.

A snail on a skateboard zooms by without care,
Chasing a butterfly, just seeing if it's fair.
The world is a stage, in the verdant abyss,
Where laughter and antics never go amiss.

So take a bold peek into this greenery filled,
With chuckles and giggles, your spirit's fulfilled.
For in every twist of the path that you roam,
You'll find joy and laughter, and always come home.

## Melody of the Moonlit Moss

Beneath the big moon, on a blanket of green,
Is where all the critters hold parties unseen.
With fireflies as dancers, their glow oh so bright,
They twirl in the soft breeze, a magical sight.

The frogs play the banjo, a tune full of cheer,
While wildflowers sway, and the night creatures near.
They whisper, they giggle, in harmony's song,
Bringing all the night critters to sing along.

A raccoon in slippers taps two tiny feet,
While the hedgehogs sit back, enjoying the beat.
The blankets of moss serve as pillows for all,
As laughter and music in the night gently fall.

So if you dare wander where shadows entwine,
And find all the mirth where the shy creatures shine,
Join in on the laughter, let the fun take its course,
In the melody woven through the moonlit moss!

## **Mysteries of the Fern Fronds**

In the shadows where the ferns do sway,
A squirrel juggles nuts in a playful way.
The owls hoot laughter, as they wink,
While slugs wear hats, or so we think.

A badger tells tales of the moonlit spree,
How raccoons dance under the old oak tree.
The mushrooms giggle, they sway and glow,
While the wind whispers secrets, soft and low.

Foxes in tuxedos, high tea on the lawn,
Are debating the best way to trot on the dawn.
With cups of dew and pastries from the grass,
The humor of nature always has class.

So gather your friends for a night of cheer,
In the ferny realm where all is clear.
For every leaf hides a story or jest,
In a world so alive, that never lets rest.

## A Breeze through the Twisted Vines

Through tangled vines where shadows play,
A bunny hops by in a comical way.
With floppy ears and a twinkle in eyes,
He juggles ripe berries, much to our surprise.

A snake in sunglasses takes a sunbathe break,
While lizards debate what's the best snack to make.
Spiders weave webs that glimmer so bright,
Their dance at dusk is a whimsical sight.

Mice dressed as chefs cook up a surprise,
With acorns and grasses, it's quite the prize.
While a parrot perches, cracks jokes from a tree,
Laughing so hard, it can hardly be free.

So wander and wander where the laughter is loud,
Amongst the twisted vines, be merry and proud.
For every gurgle and giggle you find,
Is a secret of joy that nature's designed.

## The Lullaby of the Nightingale

Beneath the stars, the nightingale sings,
With a chirpy tune on radiant wings.
A hedgehog hums, tapping its toes,
Where the daisies bloom and the sweet breeze blows.

The fireflies twinkle, a radiant light,
Leading the way through the whispering night.
A cat wears a tie and sings out of tune,
While the moon joins in with a silver croon.

The raccoons are plotting a midnight feast,\nWith
sandwiches stacked, they've invited the least.
A frog croaks loudly, he thinks he can lead,
The most curious creatures to a night-time feed.

So let the lullaby carry you away,
To where dreams are woven in playful display.
For under the gaze of a shimmery sky,
All creatures unite for a joyful goodbye.

## Celestial Paths through the Woodlands

In the woodlands where the stars waltz bright,
A bear in pajamas dances with delight.
With each clumsy step, the leaves scatter wide,
As the owls hoot along, all filled with pride.

Squirrels on scooters zoom past the trees,
Chasing the shadows and buzzing with glee.
A wise old turtle, with stories to share,
Sits under the starlight, without a care.

The hedgehogs debate what's the best berry,
While a dancing fox spins, oh so merry.
Moths in tuxedos take flight in the air,
With each flutter and flap, they bring magic to spare.

So take a stroll down these celestial trails,
Where laughter and mischief dance in the gales.
For nature's own comedy provides a grand show,
In the woodlands where humor and friendship will grow.

## Song of the Sylvan Spirits

In a thicket of laughter, the whispers play,
Squirrels debate how to steal acorns today.
Bouncing and chirping, all creatures align,
They plot silly pranks over sweet porcupine wine.

The owls wear glasses, pretending to read,
While rabbits gossip on their hops and their speed.
A hedgehog performs with a twig as his cane,
Underneath the bright moon, they dance in the rain.

Mice juggle berries, what a comical sight!
The buzzing of bees joins the musical night.
With a flip and a flop, all the fun will commence,
In this woodland of giggles, who needs any sense?

So gather the fireflies, let the night glow,
Join in the chorus, let your spirits flow.
In the realm of the wild, where laughter is free,
The song of the sylvan spirits is key.

## The Hidden Grove's Heartbeat

In the heart of the grove, there's a beat so absurd,
A frog with a drumstick, it strums and it spurred.
Beetles do breakdance, a sight to behold,
While ladybugs giggle, their secrets unfold.

The rustle of leaves sings a tune out of turn,
As the wily old fox gives his tail a good burn.
"Keep it down, keep it down!" protests the wise hare,
But they all laugh aloud, not a worry or care.

A turtle moves slowly, but he's part of the fun,
With a shell as a slide, watch them all one by one.
The chipmunks are cheering, "Come on, take a chance!"
In the hidden grove's heartbeat, they all join the dance.

With chuckles and chortles, the night carries on,
Till the sun peeks in gently, announcing the dawn.
Yet the tales of the grove, full of giggles and cheer,
Will linger and echo for all of the year.

## Legends of the Leafy Realm

In the leafy realm where the oddities play,
A snail rides a cat, 'The King of the Day!'
They race through the flowers, a wild chase ensues,
While the flowers just giggle in colorful hues.

The wise old crow tells the stories of yore,
Of mice that built castles from pebbles and shore.
And the pigeons, they hover, not wanting to miss,
The antics of foxes, is this pure bliss?

A turtle with glasses narrates with great flair,
Of the time that the beavers formed a big square.
"We built a great dam!" they announce with a cheer,
Not knowing the river was planning a steer.

In the leafy realm where laughter's the test,
All the creatures gather, they banter and jest.
Each tale shares a chuckle, each moment a grin,
In the legends of laughter, everyone wins!

## Riddles of the Ancient Trees

The ancient trees hum, with riddles quite sly,
"Why did the squirrel never tell a lie?"
With branches a-whisper, they chuckle and sway,
As the woodpecker dances and joins in the play.

"What's green and giggles?" an oak starts to tease,
"Why, it's just the moss, dancing with the breeze!"
And the owls in the glen hoot out in delight,
While the hedgehogs all tumble, they're laughing outright.

A badger named Bert, with a grin ear to ear,
Shares jokes about mushrooms all covered in beer.
The raccoons in masks fall right into line,
As they plot a new caper for stolen fish brine.

In the riddles of trees, where the joy is immense,
The laughter rings out, making perfect sense.
For when nature's in giggles, why worry or fret?
Just soak in the humor, no need for regret.

## Secrets of the Silent Spruce

In a tree where secrets dwell,
A squirrel tells tales that swell.
He claims the acorns have their say,
Their gossip brightens up the day.

The owl pretends to be quite sage,
Yet hoots at jokes from a youth's page.
The branches sway with laughter loud,
While critters dance, delighting the crowd.

The woodpecker taps a rhythm neat,
Singing praises to his tasty treat.
Each nut and berry, a story bold,
Of mischievous games never told.

So if you stroll by the silent spruce,
Listen close, you'll find the juice.
For giggles shared in the hues of green,
Are the finest tales ever seen.

## The Enchanted Underbrush

In the underbrush where shadows play,
A rabbit spun yarns at the end of the day.
With a flick of his ear and a wink of his eye,
He claims the carrots can actually fly!

The hedgehog pipes up, rolling with glee,
"Let's have a party, just you and me!"
With tiny hats and a cake shaped like leaves,
They danced in delight as the night weaves.

A sly fox then crept, full of mischief and fun,
He tried to outsmart them, all just for a pun.
But tripped on a twig, oh what a sight,
His blunders made everyone laugh with delight!

So join the dance in the enchanted glade,
Where laughter and joy are readily laid.
In the underbrush where odd tales birth,
Even the quiet ones find their worth.

## **Tales from the Twisted Roots**

Beneath the tree with roots so crooked,
Lies a toad who is often too kooky.
He tells of treasures buried deep,
And laughs until he's lost in sleep.

The bunny hops in, trying to boast,
"Listen close to my new funny toast!"
He spills his drink, what a sight to see,
And all critters giggle, hapless and free.

A raccoon shows up with shiny baubles,
Claiming they're gifts from magical gobbles.
"Just don't ask how I got them all,"
They swarm around, in jest, they enthrall.

So gather round, beneath twisted boughs,
For tales that inspire giggles and wow!
In this forest of jesters, every day,
Is a chance to laugh and play, play, play!

## **Echoes of the Elder Grove**

In the grove where the elders dwell,
The trees drop wisdom, their bark does tell.
A parrot squawks jokes, brightening the day,
As whispers of laughter float far away.

The tortoise tells of races won,
Though everyone knows he rarely runs.
The tales of his speed are met with a grin,
As leaves rustle softly in the breeze's spin.

The mischievous raccoon with a mask on his face,
Steals socks from the lines, what a hectic race!
He spins grand tales of a sock thief's plight,
Turning night into day with laughter so bright.

So visit the grove where echoes abound,
Where the silliest tales create joy all around.
For in this green kingdom, each leaf above,
Holds stories of friendship and buckets of love.

## Mossy Tales of the ancients

In a forest deep where the shadows play,
Ancient trees tell tales in a comical way.
A squirrel in a suit and a mouse in a tie,
    Debate over nuts, oh my, oh my!

The owl wears glasses, thinks he's so wise,
But forgets his own name right before our eyes.
The toads croak along, with a rhythm so sweet,
    Ribbiting jokes at a lunchtime treat.

The raccoon, he dances, with style and flair,
While the hedgehog hums, not a worry or care.
In moss-covered corners, with laughter they blend,
    Where silliness thrives and fun has no end.

So listen, dear friend, to the jesters' delight,
In the magical woods, where day turns to night.
With giggles and grins, they weave their own spell,
    In tales of the ancients, oh how they compel!

## Lessons from the Land of Leaf

In the land where leaves tumble high in the air,
A snail once declared, 'Life's just not fair!'
To all of his friends, who were laughing so loud,
He slid in a puddle, feeling quite proud.

The butterflies giggle, their colors so bright,
While ants march in lines, making sure all is right.
They teach us that laughter can lighten the load,
As long as you wear shoes when you cross the old road.

In a dance-off of flowers, the daisies won first,
While sunflowers groaned, 'Oh, what a bad thirst!'
But a bee flew on by, with a chuckle and buzz,
'Take nectar from fun, that's the true heart of fuzz!'

So remember, brave heart, from this leafy retreat,
Keep laughter close by, it's a trick that's so sweet.
In lessons of joy, under sun or moonbeam,
The true gift of life is to laugh and to dream!

## A Whisper through the Wilderness

In the whispering woods, where secrets unfold,
Lies a tale of a bear who was brash and bold.
With a hat on his head and a grin on his face,
He tried dancing swiftly, but fell with no grace.

A fox with a grin shared a wise little trick,
'When you trip on your paws, just roll like a brick!'
The deer joined in, with a jump and a skip,
While the rabbits all laughed till they almost flipped.

The trees swayed in rhythm, their branches did sway,
As the creatures all gathered for a woodland ballet.
With giggles and chatter, they spun through the night,
In whispers of laughter, oh, wasn't it bright?

So venture, dear friend, through the wild of the green,
Where the joy is contagious, and fun can be seen.
In the whispers of wilderness, secrets abound,
With laughter and cheer, true magic is found!

## The Twilight Trials of Nature

In the twilight of nature, where shadows embark,
A turtle named Tim found a glow-in-the-dark.
With a wink and a nod, he said, "This is neat!
Now I'll be faster! Just watch my quick feet!"

But the rabbits just giggled, with twitches of cheer,
"The glow isn't magic! Have another root beer!"
They planned a race down to the old willow tree,
While Tim made excuses, quite humorously.

When the twilight turned golden, they took off so fast,
Tim trailed far behind, as they flew over grass.
But soon he discovered, in the joy of the chase,
That laughter's the winner in this silly race.

So join in the trials where nature will jest,
With friends by your side, you'll always be blessed.
In twilight's warm glow, let giggles take flight,
For in nature's embrace, there's pure joy tonight!

www.ingramcontent.com/pod-product-compliance
Lightning Source LLC
Chambersburg PA
CBHW072140200426
43209CB00052IB/187